Contents

First English edition 1980
Macdonald Educational Ltd.
Holywell House
Worship Street
London EC2A 2EN

ISBN 0 356 06754 8

Printed in Italy by
A. Mondadori, Verona

Engine Drivers

of the great steam trains

by MELVILLE WALLACE
illustrated by MICHAEL TURNER

Macdonald Educational

Around the world by steam

Above: Steam power on land and sea. A boat train pulls up on the quayside allowing passengers to transfer straight on to the White Star liner tied up alongside.

Right: In 1937 a Humber Snipe beat the Orient Express in a race from Istanbul to Ostende.

1

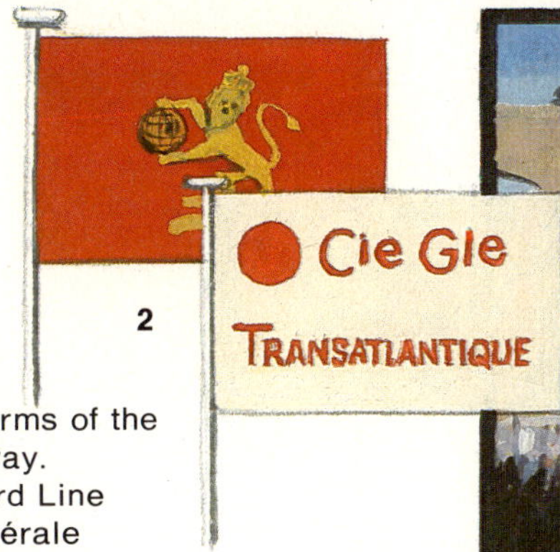

2

3

4

Above: 1. Coats of arms of the Great Western Railway. 2. Flags of the Cunard Line and Compagnie Générale Transatlantique. 3. Poster advertising the Blue Train. 4. Timetable of the Wagon-Lits company.

If Jules Verne had waited a few more years to write his best-seller *Around the World in Eighty Days* he could have reduced the time to 40 days. Leaving his London club promptly at 10.30 a.m. the hero, Phineas Fogg, could have walked to Victoria Station in time to catch the Golden Arrow at 11 o'clock sharp. A little over three hours later, descending the gangplank of the cross-Channel ferry *Canterbury,* he would have found the Nord Express waiting to carry him on to Liège, Hanover, Berlin and Riga on the Baltic. There he would have had to change to a broad-gauge Russian train to take him on to Moscow.

Only 72 hours after setting out, Fogg could have been about to leave Moscow aboard the Trans-Siberian express. After eight days and 18 engine changes he would have reached the frontier town of Zabayakalsk where he would have transferred to the Trans-Manchurian for the run across Manchuria to the Russian port of Vladivostok. After a brief interlude on the Sea of Japan and a short trip across the island of Honshu, he would have been in Yokohama. From there a luxurious liner of the US President or Dollar Lines would have carried him over the Pacific to San Francisco's Golden Gate. A crack Union Pacific express, the Overland, would take him to Chicago in a little over three days, and less than 24 hours aboard the 20th Century Limited would have found him in New York. As a British subject, Fogg would naturally have chosen the Cunard Line's *Berengaria* or *Mauretania* for the trip home. He could have had an equally comfortable voyage aboard the *Ile de France* or North German Lloyd's *Bremen* or *Europa,* the fastest ships afloat. In any case, four and a half days later he would have docked at Southampton to be met by a special boat train. This would have whisked him non-stop to London and his club. The round-the-world voyage of over 30,000 kilometres would have taken less than 40 days – all of it by steam power and two-thirds of it by rail.

The Age of Steam, which had begun in 1712 with Newcomen's primitive pumping engine, reached a peak over two centuries later in the years between the two World Wars. Cars were no longer a novelty but they were used mainly for local trips. The airlines had started to spread their networks across the world but inter-city flight was still something of an adventure. For long journeys trains were still the fastest, safest, most dependable and most comfortable means of travel. Nevertheless competition from these new forms of transport spurred railwaymen everywhere to improve tracks, redesign engines and tighten schedules in an effort to keep the railways' position as the world's foremost means of travel.

The locomotive

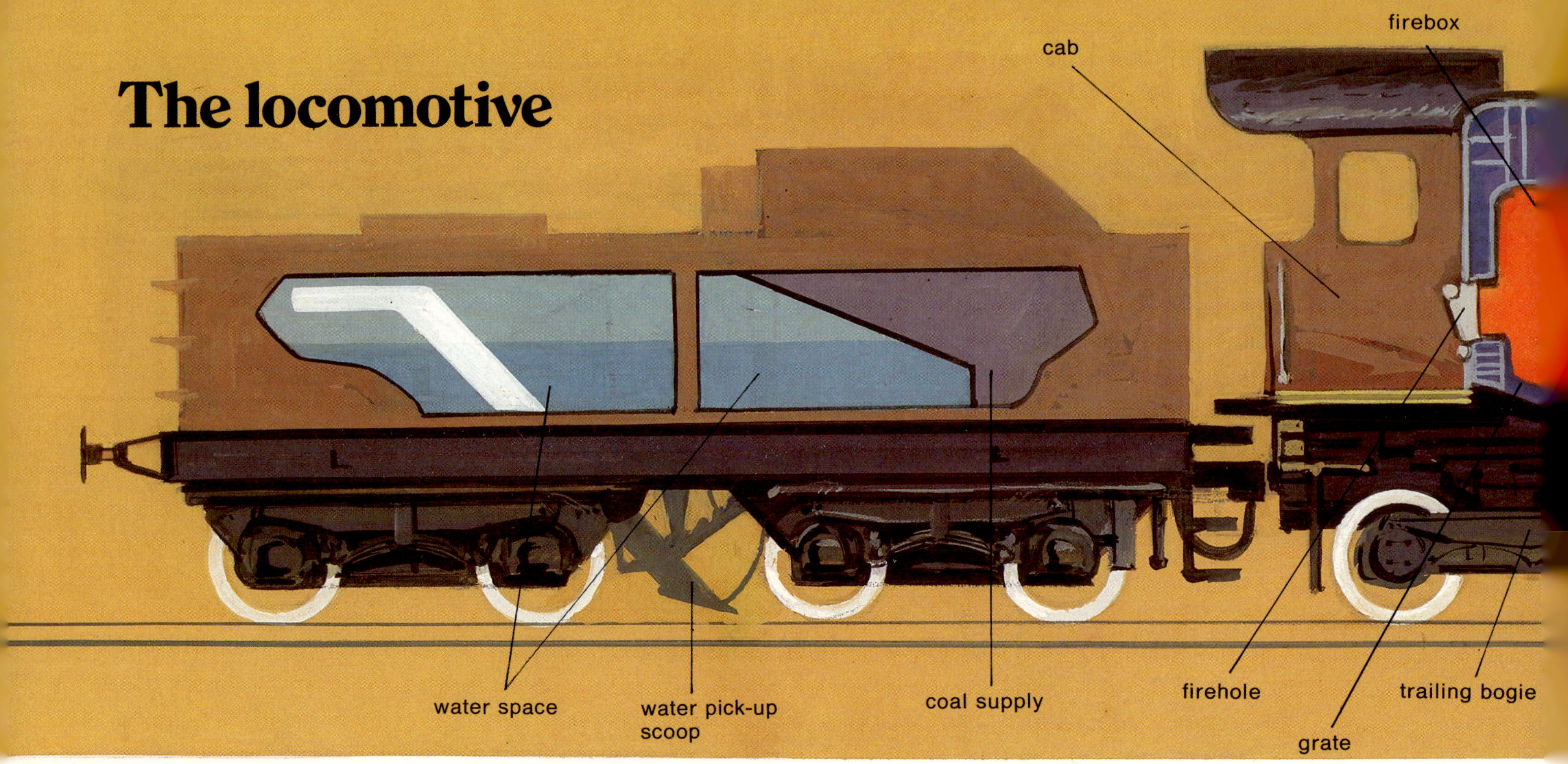

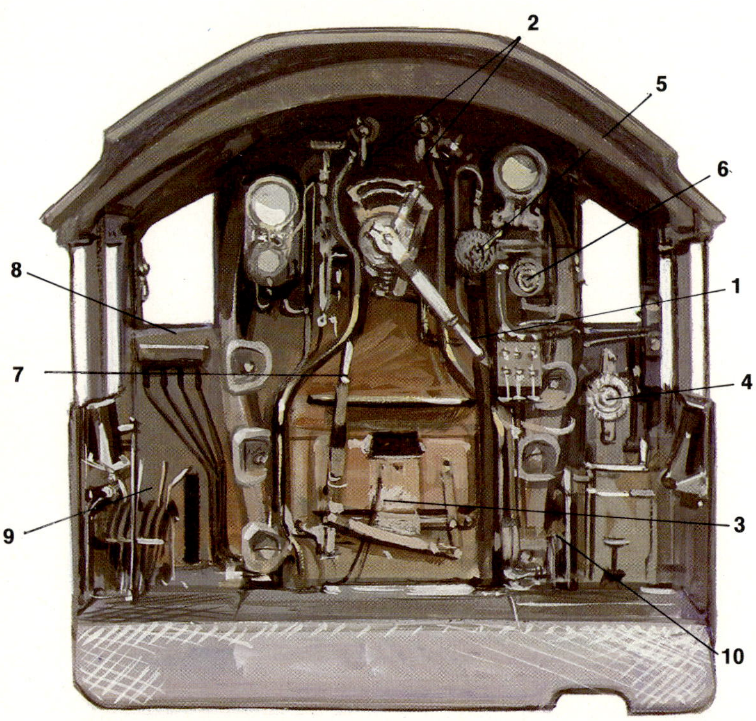

Above: 1. Regulator. 2. Steam valves for injectors.
3. Firehole. 4. Reversing-gear handle. 5. Brake application handle. 6. Blower valve.
7. Firehole door and lever.
8. Oil boxes. 9. Damper controls. 10. Cylinder cock control.

A steam locomotive essentially consists of two parts. The first part, which turns water into high-pressure steam, is made up of the firebox, boiler and smokebox. The second part consists of the valve gear, cylinders, rods and wheels which drive the locomotive forward. Large locomotives also have a separate tender which carries its supplies of fuel and water.

Briefly, an engine works this way. Water is normally taken into the tender from an overhead supply. From there it is fed into the boiler by injectors which are activated by steam from the locomotive itself. Fuel from the tender is thrown, shovelled or injected (depending on whether wood, coal or oil is being used) on to the grate where it is burned. The air required to keep the fire going flows up through dampers below the grate. Flame and smoke from the fire then pass through a cluster of long fire-tubes set in the cylindrical boiler. They give up their heat to the water before passing out through the smokebox and up the chimney. The water boils and forms steam, which rises to the top of the boiler, where it is collected in the dome. After passing through the regulator it goes into the superheater which raises both its temperature and pressure still further.

The high-pressure steam then passes directly to the valves which admit it to the cylinders. Steam is applied to each side of the piston in turn so that power is produced on both the forward and reverse strokes. The

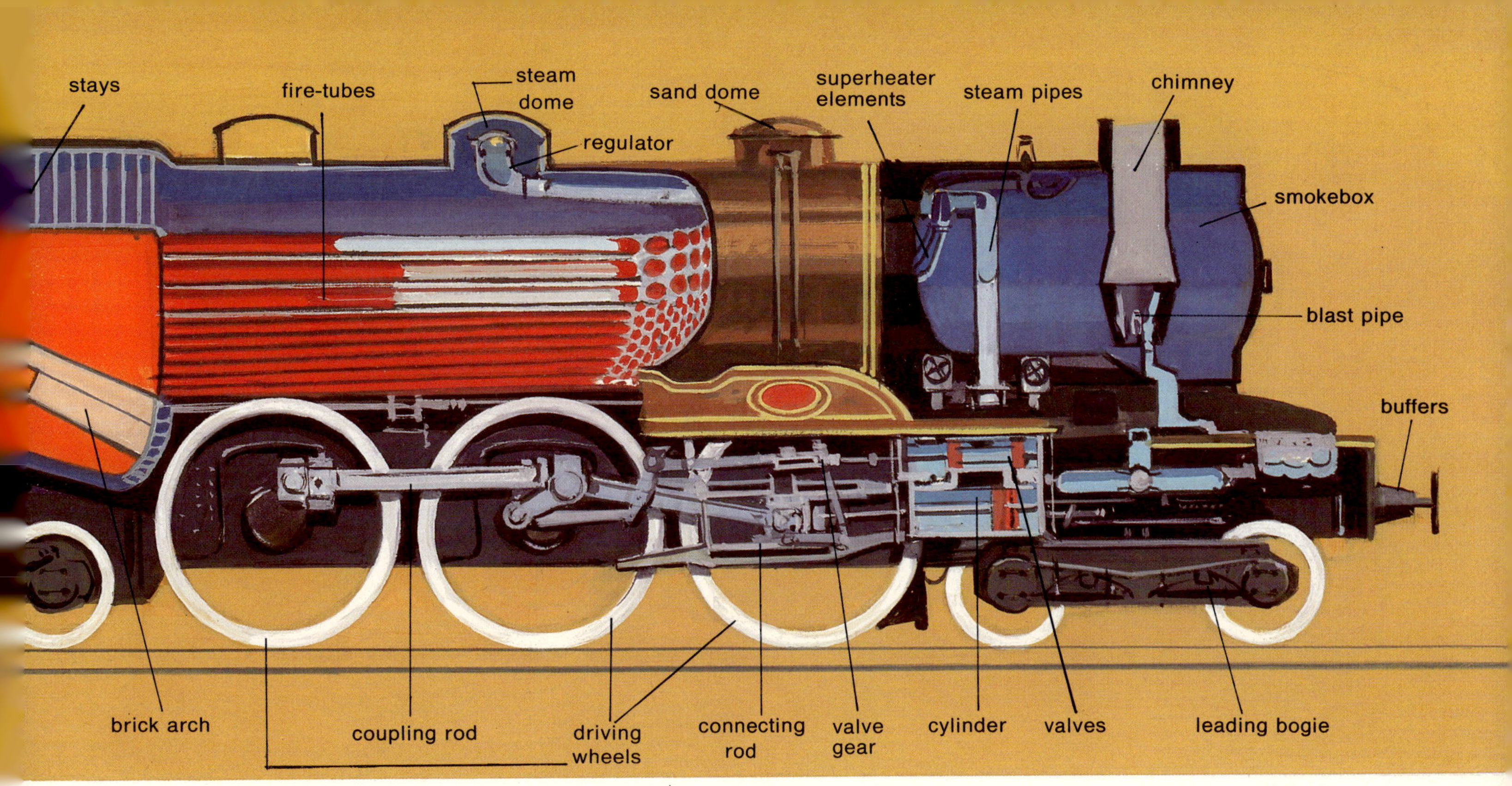

valve linkage is so arranged that steam is only admitted during part of the piston's stroke. In this way the most is made of the steam's power to expand. After being exhausted from the cylinders the steam passes through one or more jets in the smokebox and creates a vacuum which sucks air through the fire-tubes. This increased draught raises the rate of combustion and improves the engine's steaming capacity.

The engine driver has two basic controls to work with. The regulator varies the amount of steam leaving the boiler, while the valve gear controls the proportion of the stroke during which it is admitted to the cylinders. When starting, for instance, continuous pressure is required over the full stroke, but too much steam pressure could result in the locomotive spinning its wheels. At full speed, on the other hand, efficient running depends on using steam at full pressure but admitting it only during part of the stroke.

Though this basic arrangement has remained unchanged, many improvements in locomotive design have been made over the years to increase power and efficiency. Fireboxes were re-modelled to cope with specific types of fuel, and the ratio of grate area to boiler size was modified to raise steaming capacity. Experiments have also been tried with different kinds of exhaust systems and different valves including slide, piston and poppet types.

One of the most successful ways of getting maximum power from expanding steam was the system of compounding introduced by Mallet and used extensively on the French railways. In this arrangement high-pressure steam goes first to one set of cylinders and then to a second pair of low-pressure cylinders before being exhausted through the chimney. On compound engines the smaller, high-pressure cylinders were often placed between the frame and connected to one pair of driving wheels through a cranked axle. The low-pressure cylinders were mounted outside and powered a different pair of wheels, although all the driving wheels were connected together. Compound engines remained popular in continental Europe for many years but were abandoned earlier in the United States and Britain.

Peak steam locomotive efficiency was undoubtedly achieved by France's André Chapelon. Taking an old Pacific, he virtually doubled its power output by increasing the superheating, and enlarging and streamlining the steam ducts leading to the cylinders. He used a modification of the Finnish engineer Kyläla's exhaust system which greatly increased draught. The new exhaust system was named 'Kylchap'.

Some express locomotives were fitted with a scoop which could be lowered into a long, narrow water trough between the rails. This allowed them to take up water while on the move.

1

Purpose-built machines

In the early days of railways the same engines were used to haul heavy mineral wagons and passenger trains. However it soon became clear that there were advantages in designing locomotives for specific tasks. Powerful engines were needed to haul heavy freight trains and to tackle steep inclines in mountainous country. Increasing the number of driving wheels produced locomotives suited to this work. This arrangement increased the engines' pulling power as the increased weight on the driving wheels reduced their tendency to slip. Heavy engines could run over light track if their weight was distributed over several axles.

For each revolution a large wheel makes it covers more ground than a small one. Large driving wheels therefore allow greater speeds to be achieved for the same piston travel. The nineteenth-century British engineer Thomas Crampton was working on this principle when he patented a design for a fast passenger locomotive which had a single pair of rear-mounted driving wheels over 2.5 metres in diameter. The more usual approach was to increase the number of driving wheels to four or six to give greater adhesion and stability. Nevertheless high-speed passenger locomotives continued to follow the large-wheel principle. The huge Atlantic built in America in 1936 to power the crack 160 km/h Hiawatha had wheels 2.18 metres across.

On shorter commuter runs, or for shunting duties where an engine was never very far from its home base, a tender could be more of a hindrance than a help. Engines designed for short-distance work therefore carried fuel and water supplies on their own frames. They were known as tank engines. A small coal bunker was normally mounted behind the cab, and water was carried in tanks mounted on either side of the boiler. Shunting engines ran at low speed but needed maximum adhesion. To achieve this, the whole weight was often carried on the driving wheels which were mounted directly on the frame without coupling axles.

Railways in developing countries frequently included sections of unstable track, sharp curves and long distances between refuelling points. In many cases articulated engines were the solution to the problems which this caused. In the system invented by the Swiss

2

3

Left: 1. An oil-fired 2-10-4 of the Canadian Pacific which weighed 330 tons. 2. A 4-4-4 high-speed passenger locomotive of the Baltimore and Ohio railway. 3. The Garratt model which was used on lines throughout Africa.

Below: A 2-6-4-T locomotive which hauled suburban and local services on Britain's Southern Railway. The letter 'T' distinguishes tank engines from engines with tenders.

engineer Anatole Mallet a high-pressure engine was mounted on a swivelling bogie at the front while a set of low-pressure cylinders drove normal fixed wheels positioned under the rear end of the boiler and cab. Britain's Herbert Garratt produced an articulated design which consisted essentially of two separate engines taking steam from a common boiler slung between them. These locomotives' low axle loadings and high flexibility made them safe and dependable on even the most treacherous track. The huge tenders above each engine unit gave them tremendous range. Garratt locomotives were adapted to all gauges and climates, hauling passenger expresses in Algeria and ore trains in Central Africa and South America.

Left: A century of locomotive development separates the tiny *Rocket* from the huge *Big Boy*. The Chapelon 4-8-0 standing between them produced two-thirds as much power as the *Big Boy*.

Right: The Union Pacific's 350-ton *Big Boy*. This 4-8-8-4 Mallet design developed over 6,000 hp.

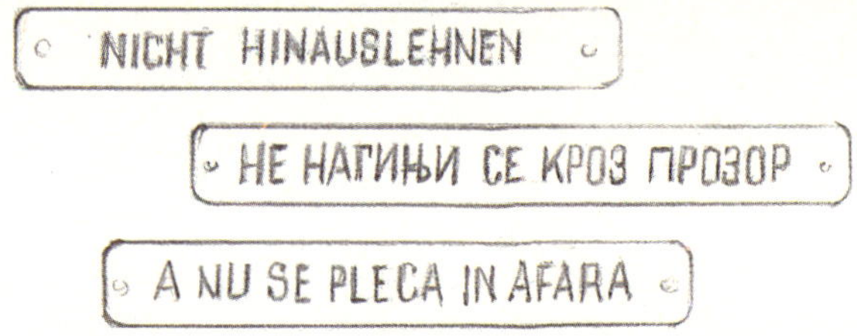

Left: Coats of arms of the Wagon-Lits and Pullman companies decorated the coaches.

Above: Different languages with the same message: 'Do not lean out of the window.'

Setting out

Steam locomotives could not simply be started up and driven away. Before the drivers and firemen arrived on duty the 'lighter' went round the shed kindling the fires in the grates of all the locomotives. It was a tricky job as each locomotive has its individual quirks. At the same time an apprentice wiped grime from the paintwork and polished the brass fittings.

The driver and firemen, the most highly skilled men in the shed, clocked on an hour before departure time. They carefully inspected their locomotive from top to bottom and checked all the controls and gauges before getting down to work. It was the fireman's job to bring the steam in the boiler up to the required pressure. The driver got out his long-spouted oil can and began to lubricate the moving parts. Oil cups on the axles and connecting rods had to be filled to the brim. A squirt of oil was applied to every piston, valve and moving part of the valve motion. Neither too much nor too little was used, for oil consumption was carefully recorded. With these preparations complete, the crew inched the locomotive on to the turntable. There it was swivelled into position for the siding on which it could pick up water, sand and coal.

At the coaling stop there was sometimes an argument between the fireman and the yard workers. The footplatemen always wanted the best coal for the needs and dignity of their machine. Really bad coal could block the tubes, stifle the fire or even go up the flue without burning. Some types were full of pebbles or formed a sticky, glowing clinker on the grate which had to be raked away to keep the fire burning properly. Not only was this wasteful but the delay caused by the drop in steam pressure made it difficult to stay on schedule. The footplate crews were held responsible for any time lost.

Meanwhile, shunting engines were assembling the train. Each coupling and hose connection was double-checked and the outside of the coaches was thoroughly scrubbed with brushes, soap and steam. They had already been swept and cleaned inside. Reservation stubs were fitted into the little brass frames beside each compartment. Finally the sign-boards were fixed to the side of each carriage announcing its ultimate destination.

Consulting his watch, the driver waited for a signal to leave the shed. After a short journey to the terminus he gently backed his locomotive on to the waiting train, which had already been brought there by the shunting engine. Standing down on the tracks beneath the coaches the shunter coupled up the locomotive to the coaches, fitted the brake pipes and checked the system. All was then ready for departure.

Above: To avoid unnecessary movements in crowded depot yards, locomotives often stood in circular or fan-shaped buildings called roundhouses. A star-shaped pattern of tracks led from the sheds to a central turntable from which they could easily be dispatched in any direction.

Left: Before each journey the carriages were thoroughly cleaned inside and out.

The Orient Express

Below: Trunks and packing cases are stowed aboard the luggage van as the Simplon-Orient express waits to leave the Gare de Lyon, Paris. On the next platform an express has just arrived behind a conical-nosed locomotive of the Paris-Lyon-Marseilles railway. Though it looks as though it was designed primarily for speed, its eight driving wheels were only 1.8 metres in diameter so that it could haul heavy trains over the hills of the Cote d'Or in Burgundy. Locomotives of this type frequently hauled the Simplon-Orient express on the first leg of its journey to Basle.

Every evening the blue coaches of the Simplon-Orient express were drawn up at the Gare de Lyons, Paris, waiting to start their long journey east. While diplomats and adventurers were settling themselves in their well-appointed compartments the driver and fireman made last-minute checks. Precisely on time the right-away whistle blew. The driver made sure that the signals showed all-clear, and the famous train slowly pulled out of the station en route for Istanbul.

The idea for a through luxury train service across Europe came from Georges Nagelmackers, the Belgian founder of the Wagon-Lits company. It took him years of difficult negotiation with privately owned railways and the governments of the seven countries on the route before the first Orient Express covered the 3,000 kilometres from Paris to the Black Sea in 1883. At that time the train left from the Gare de L'Est and its route was via Strasbourg, across southern Germany to Munich, then across the Austrian border at Salzburg and on to Vienna. From there it went through Budapest, Bucharest until it reached the Black Sea at Varna. Passengers for Istanbul continued their journey by steamer.

Despite blizzards and bandits and the ups and downs of Balkan politics this service continued until the First World War. At the end of the war the Treaty of Versailles specified that the Orient Express must run again. Meanwhile a new route had been opened through Switzerland's Simplon tunnel to Milan. The train then went on to Venice, Trieste and Belgrade, capital of the newly independent state of Yugoslavia, before continuing on to Bulgaria and the East. Some sleeping and dining car crews worked the entire route.

Engine changes were frequent and each country supplied its own footplate crew. Passengers had to go through customs and passport formalities at every border. Bulgaria always raised problems for the trains' international crews and it became a nightmare on the occasions when King Boris decided he wanted to drive the express. Decked out in a dazzling white driver's outfit produced by his Paris tailor, he took over the train as soon as it reached the Bulgarian frontier.

The railway community

Railways were complicated operations which not only carried the bulk of the world's freight but also delivered passengers to every corner of six continents. The railway companies had to employ huge numbers of manual workers and office staff. Their skills were as varied as those of a wine-steward or foundry worker, conductor or boilermaker, reservation clerk or signalman. From the grandest station master to the youngest cleaner in the sheds, they all felt themselves to be part of the great railway community.

Every major terminal was the nerve centre for the organization responsible for running a section of the railway. It bustled with office and administrative workers who maintained contact with outlying stations, routed freight wagons, scheduled extra sections of fast expresses when required and ensured that spare locomotives were available in case of emergency. Baggage

Above: The smart uniforms of the guards, ticket collectors and inspectors were all part of the military-style discipline of the railways. Special caps and badges of office indicated what job their wearers were doing. The highest-ranking members of staff had the most splendid uniforms. Station masters used to make quite a ceremony of greeting any VIP who was passing through their station.

Right: It was a matter of pride that the trains should always run on time. In railway families gold pocket watches were handed down from one generation to the next. The guard's whistle and the station-announcer's megaphone were small but essential pieces of equipment. The smart brown cap of the Wagon-Lits company's sleeping-car attendant matched the uniform worn by all Wagon-Lits employees.

had to be properly checked in and accounted for. Express parcels were delivered or forwarded in transit. Passengers were supplied with information about the times of their trains. A stentorian-voiced announcer had to stand by the platforms and sing out the destination of every departing train so that passengers did not board the wrong one by mistake. Even the smallest country station needed its own station master and an assistant to cope with these round-the-clock operations.

The railway companies relied on a hierarchy of jobs which was modelled on the army. Every job had its own grade and rank, and staff who came into contact with the public always wore a special uniform. Distinctive colours, badges and emblems all marked out senior staff from the juniors. Pullman porters welcomed their passengers aboard with a salute. The smart brown uniforms of the attendants on the Wagon-Lits sleeping cars became a hallmark of the comfort and service which that company provided.

A special sense of community existed among the manual workers who drove or maintained the locomotives, assembled freight trains in the marshalling yards or controlled the traffic from the signal boxes.

Below: The driver's cap and goggles and the univeral little black case which went with him on every journey.

Above: The footplate crews had their own 'uniform' of dark, grimy overalls and added an individual touch with their brightly coloured scarves and hats. The drivers usually wore goggles to protect their eyes from dust and soot.

Their jobs were hard and dirty so an elegant uniform would have been quite out of place. They wore blue or grey overalls to protect themselves from the dirt, often with a brightly coloured scarf around their necks to keep out the soot and ash. The footplatemen themselves were perhaps the proudest of all. They made sure that their special skills were recognized through their own trade unions which bargained hard to maintain their special privileges.

The railway workers and their families lived a life apart from the non-railway community. Often they inhabited rows of small brick cottages or barrack-like blocks of flats and boarding houses 'on the other side of the tracks'. Forced by the railways' schedules to work irregular shifts, the population of these settlements was always astir. At 3 a.m., while the rest of the city slept, the 'caller' was trotting down the street knocking up the engine crews who were scheduled for an early departure. A fireman might be picking up his lunch basket while in a neighbouring home hot water flowed into a tub for a returning driver's much-needed bath. Railway families spent many of their off-duty hours on the plots allocated to them on unoccupied land next to the sidings. On these tiny allotments they grew many of the fruit and vegetables they needed. The children played nearby and formed friendships that could last a lifetime – all in the railway community.

4353

Above: Like the airliners of today, many steam locomotives had their 'black boxes' which recorded the speed over every section of track. Sometimes there were electrical connections to the signals sounding an alarm in the cab which had to be cancelled by the driver or fireman.

Below: Water was poured into the tender from an overhead crane during a five-minute station stop. The driver usually handled the valve gear at the base of the crane while the fireman stood on the tender and directed the water into the tank. Locomotives on certain lines were fitted with a scoop which could be lowered into long water troughs mounted between the tracks along certain sections of the route. This arrangement allowed the tender to be refilled with water while the train was in motion.

Learning the trade

Every locomotive carried a crew of two – a driver and a fireman. While the driver took final responsibility, the fireman's job was equally important. It was up to him to supply the steam which powered the locomotive.

With one eye on the water-level indicators and the other on the steam pressure gauges, the fireman worked the injectors to keep the boiler well filled with water from the tender. Then, balancing on the rocking footplate, he flipped the firebox door open with his shovel and covered the grate with an even layer of coal. One shovel-full went into each corner, one to the centre of the grate and a couple more to the area just under the door. Every hour the fireman had to shovel in several tons of coal.

Like the driver, the fireman had to know every millimetre of the track ahead. Every incline needed a little extra power and every downhill stretch meant less coal to shovel. On some railways both members of the team were paid a bonus if they saved on coal. There was the danger of a blow-back to avoid too. In the enclosed space of a tunnel, or when the driver had to close down the regulator, a draught of air down the chimney could blow back through the fire-tubes and shoot a searing flame into the cab if precautions were not taken to prevent it.

Conversation was almost impossible in the cab because of the noise of the exhaust, the rattle of the footplate and the pounding of the great driving wheels. Nevertheless the two crew men learned to understand each other perfectly.

Being a fireman was a step on the path to becoming a driver. Young boys who joined the railway company as apprentices usually started in the yards and sheds. There they scraped clinkers from the grate and cleaned soot from the smokebox. After several years of this unrewarding work the apprentice was boosted into the cab and handed a shovel. In the company of an older and experienced driver he learnt the fireman's craft. Inexperienced firemen usually started in the cab of a shunter and then graduated to goods, slow passenger and finally express trains. After years of this arduous on-the-job training, and having memorized the company's rules and regulations, he was finally given his own engine to drive.

The driver's skills

Below: American locomotives were fitted with a bell. It was used at level crossings or if animals were on the line.

The steam locomotive was a powerful machine, but it needed a sensitive hand on the controls to get the most out of it. The driver, fireman and locomotive formed an inseparable trio, but only the driver was allowed to touch the main controls – the regulator, the valve gear and the brakes. In addition he kept a constant watch on the water-level gauges and the two indicators showing steam pressure in the boiler and in the steam chest, where it was admitted into the cylinders.

On hearing the 'right-away' whistle from the guard or station master he gently eased up on the regulator. With a hiss of steam and a blast of smoke the engine's great driving wheels started to turn and the express was on its way. A driver needed to know his engine's pulling capacity as well as the weight of the train. Too much regulator applied too suddenly would simply spin the engine's wheels without any progress being made. He made further adjustments to regulator and valve gear as the train inched out of the station and across the points before gaining momentum on the main line. When running at cruising speed the driver held the regulator wide open but reduced the valve travel so that steam was only admitted to the cylinders for about 25% of the piston stroke. In this way full use was made of the power of expansion of the steam.

Keeping the train moving was not the driver's only concern. Leaning out of the cab window with one hand constantly on the regulator, and the brake lever within easy reach, he peered ahead at the signals and speed indicators. He had to be ready to slow down for every restricted curve, bridge and station. If a red light showed ahead he had to be able to stop the train in time.

The air brake perfected by George Westinghouse late in the nineteenth century became standard equipment on rolling stock in America. In Britain and the Continent some railways used the Westinghouse system while others used vacuum brakes. This lack of standardization meant that rolling stock which worked through had to be equipped for both systems. The Orient Express had to switch back and forth as three countries along its route employed compressed air and another three the vacuum system.

Westinghouse system

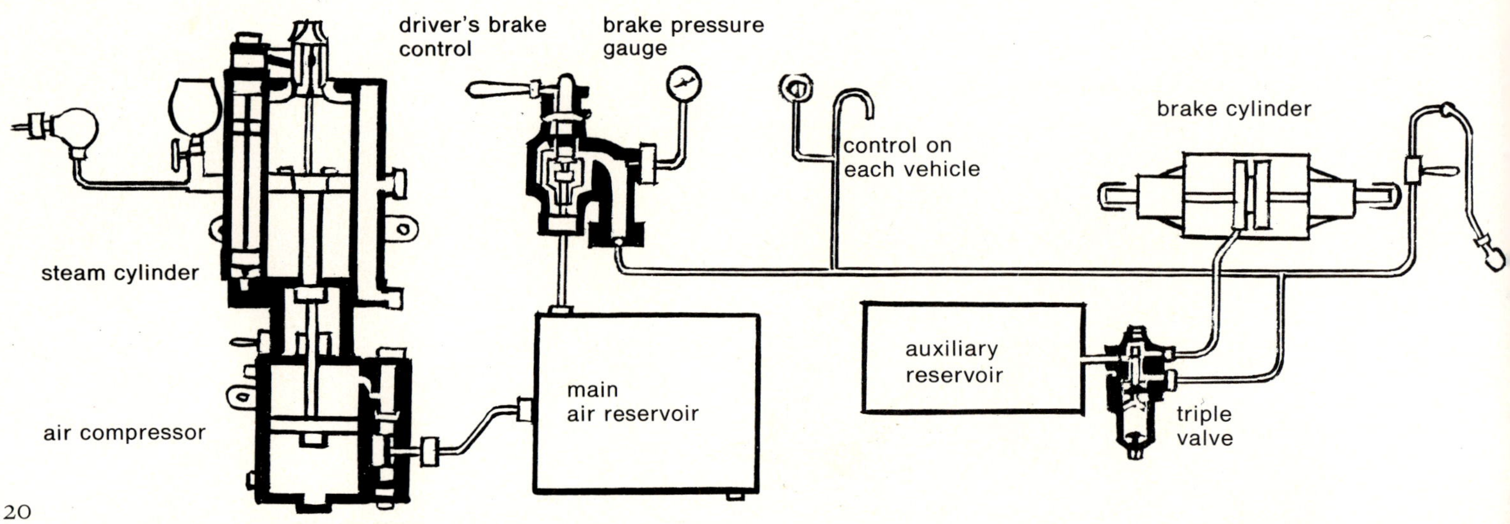

Westinghouse's arrangement was ingenious but simple. A steam-driven compressor and main air reservoir were mounted on the locomotive. Each carriage had an auxiliary reservoir, a triple valve and a brake cylinder, and was connected to the main reservoir by a pipe running the length of the train. When the driver operated the brake lever, the pressure in the train pipe was reduced. This activated the triple valve, which released compressed air from the auxiliary reservoir into the brake cylinder. The compressed air forced the piston forward to apply the brake shoe against each wheel. This system provided smooth braking along the whole train. Furthermore the brakes could be operated from anywhere in the train, for example by the guard using the emergency brake. If a carriage or wagon became uncoupled, pressure in the train pipe dropped immediately and the train was automatically brought to a halt. This 'fail-safe' feature was immensely important and was a prime factor in reducing railway accidents.

Right: As well as keeping the locomotive running the driver had to keep watch out of the side window for signals or obstructions ahead.

Signals and shunting

Complex scheduling and signalling arrangements were needed to keep the expresses on the move to their destinations. With slow local trains, fast freights and luxury expresses all using the same lines, careful controls and strict organization were needed to prevent chaos and collisions. The signalman's basic document was the working timetable which gave the precise times of each train and showed where the slower ones would have to wait in sidings to allow the others to pass. Other factors also had to be taken into account. A freight might be running slow, for instance, or a heavily loaded passenger train might have to spend more time than usual unloading at a station. Mechanical failures occurred from time to time so that re-routing or re-scheduling were required to keep the rest of the traffic moving.

An efficient signalling system was arranged to ensure that drivers had time to apply the brakes if the line ahead was blocked. Each country devised its own variation of semaphore and light signals. Whatever the system, it had to indicate 'stop', 'caution' and 'all-clear' for the section of track immediately ahead. In Britain and Germany, for instance, two-position semaphore arms were employed, with lights for use at night. Stop signals had red arms and showed a red light in the 'danger' position. The yellow fish-tailed arms were known as 'distant' signals and gave advance warning of the aspect of the next stop signal.

Two different types of light signals were developed. In the multi-lens system used in Britain and Europe there was a separate glass for each colour. The American searchlight type had an internal mechanism which changed the colour of the beam shining from a single lens. Safety on the railways was further increased with the development of track circuits and automatic train control. These could stop the train even if the driver had missed a signal and ignored the warning siren which sounded in the cab.

Marshalling yards were of great importance to a railway as it was here that freight wagons were sorted and re-assembled to form trains going to the required destination. On some railways up to 90% of the company's income came from its freight business. The basic layout was simple. As a train arrived it was held in one of the reception sidings. When the controller was ready for it the wagons were uncoupled and a shunting locomotive slowly pushed the string of trucks up the hump.

After each wagon reached the top, gravity took over as it rolled down the other side. By operating an array of points the controller directed it to any one of the sorting sidings which fanned out from the hump. The wagons which collected in each siding were then coupled together to make up the new trains. Shunters walked along the incoming train and shouted numbers to the controller telling him which siding each wagon should go to. A brakeman either rode it down the incline or applied a shoe to the track in front of the oncoming car to slow it down. Another shunter leapt between the stationary and moving cars to couple them up as soon as they met.

In more modern systems the points were operated mechanically or pneumatically from a central panel. The controller slowed the wagons by operating a remotely controlled brake called a retarder. This was a pair of pneumatically activated beams about 20 metres long which pressed against the wheel flanges.

Most engine crews found work in the marshalling yards dull and repetitive. Sometimes express drivers were disciplined by being relegated to this task. For them it was a terrible fate to have to go back to the yards, but at least it was better than being banned from the footplate for ever.

Above: Simplified layout of a marshalling yard.

Speeding the mails

Immediately behind the engine and tender came the 'head-end cars'. These were the carriages specially designed to carry mail, baggage and express parcels. Postal authorities throughout the world quickly realized the potential of the railways. As early as 1838 travelling post offices complete with pick-up and delivery apparatus were travelling between London and Liverpool. This example was soon imitated in the United States, and during the peak years of the American railways 9,000 trains carried mail over 300,000 route-kilometres. They earned the railways over $50 million per year.

All government mail contracts contained penalty clauses for delays. Mail trains were therefore given absolute priority on the track, even taking precedence over luxury expresses. Typical of British all-mail trains were the Up Special and Down Special running on tight schedules between London's Euston station and Glasgow and Aberdeen in Scotland. The usual formation for these trains was 12 carriages. Some of them were stowage vans for through mail but the rest were travelling post offices which picked up mail at intermediate stations and sorted it as the train thundered along. One difficulty with travelling post offices was that the vehicles always had to work with the pick-up apparatus on the left side of the track. Unlike ordinary carriages, which could simply be reversed for the return journey, the TPOs had to be turned around at the end of each run.

Many engine crews enjoyed working the fast mail trains. The driver had priority over other trains and had no worries about passenger comfort, so he could get the very most out of his locomotive. It was on a mail run from the west of England that the famous *City of Truro,* towing five mail vans, first topped the 100 miles per hour mark (160km/h). An equally famous all-mail train (though eventually it also carried passengers) was the India Mail. From Calais it raced the length of France and Italy to Brindisi. Here the mailbags were put aboard a P & O liner for Bombay, saving a full week's travel time on the sea journey through the Bay of Biscay.

Other typical head-end cars were devoted to baggage and express parcels. In America they were generally 18 to 20 metres long, of all-steel construction and fireproofed to counter possible insurance claims. The

Above: Mail bags from the local post office were hung on apparatus beside the track. As the train sped past, a net on the side of the train scooped it in. A similar arrangement was used to drop mail from the train into a net by the trackside.

express package business began when stage-coach drivers carried currency and other valuables in a locked chest beneath their seats.

In time the baggage and parcels car became an informal meeting place for passengers and crew. In addition to the Railway Express man at his safe or desk, off-duty Pullman porters would gather there for a quiet chat. First-class passengers came to visit their pets, and the train's conductor took a break between rounds of punching tickets. Railway regulations stated that coffins had to be accompanied, and many hard-up travellers managed to cross the North American continent at an undertaker's expense, riding free all the way in the baggage car.

Above: Post Office workers in a travelling Post Office sorting mail as the train speeds on. They had to work quickly after each pick-up to make sure that all the mail had been sorted in time for the next dropping-off point.

Open trucks and wooden coaches

Right: The wooden carriages of the USSR's 'hard' class did not provide much comfort for the passengers.

Below: The USSR followed a sensible policy of standardization in engine design. Over 2,000 of the SU class shown here were built in the 1920s and 1930s.

Railways were invented to carry coal, not people. At first the precious locomotives were reserved for heavy mineral trains but by 1830 the railway companies realized that people would pay to travel in trains hauled by steam locomotives. The first passengers rode in open wagons but the railways soon started to build special passenger coaches. They consisted of two or three compartments closely modelled on stage-coach bodies, joined together and supported by four wheels on fixed axles. The individual compartments were reached through doors in the side. It was well over half a century later, after journeys became longer, that some connection between the compartments was included. In Victorian Britain, where privacy was highly valued, the connection was made along a side corridor and each compartment kept its own door on to the platform. In sociable America the open coach was developed. It had a central aisle with seats on either side. This arrangement became standard in many parts of Germany, Eastern Europe, Scandinavia, Japan and Russia.

The most important development in carriage design was made in America where flimsy track with many sharp curves made rigid wheels both uncomfortable and dangerous. A smoother ride and greater stability were obtained by mounting each end of the carriage on a separate four-wheeled truck called a bogie. Comfort and safety were improved still further by spring-mounted wheels. An additional advantage of bogies was that long coaches could be built which would still go round tight corners. Eventually the bogie system was adopted all over the world for passenger coaches and some freight wagons.

When the American engineer Whistler (the famous painter's father) was invited to build Russia's first railway from St Petersburg (now re-named Leningrad) to Moscow he chose a 1.524-metre (5 ft) gauge. This became the standard Russian gauge from the Baltic to the Pacific. The first line was soon followed by an international link to Vienna via Warsaw. Late in the nineteenth century Russia's rail network extended from the Arctic Ocean to the Black Sea and east of the Ural mountains to Chelyabinsk, 2,000 kilometres from Moscow.

Vladivostok was still another 7,400 kilometres further east. In between there was the vast, under-

Above: The Turkestan-Siberia line between Alma-Ata and Novosibirsk was the first great rail project of the Soviet government. Its completion in 1929 was celebrated throughout the USSR.

populated territory of Siberia. Work on the Trans-Siberian railway across this inhospitable landscape began in 1891. Crews worked eastward from Chelyabinsk and westward from Vladivostok. For 13 years they struggled to link the two ends of the country. In winter they laid track over the frozen ground only to see it disappear when the spring thaws turned the surface to spongy mud. The mountains around Lake Baikal proved an almost insuperable obstacle. It took five years of effort to blast the 42 tunnels needed to get the line through. In the meantime trains travelled in winter across tracks laid on the frozen lake. In summer the journey had to be made by ferry. A short-cut was built across Manchuria but the Boxer Rebellion and war with Japan revealed its strategic weakness. The all-Russian route to Khabarovsk on the Ussuri River and then south to Vladivostok was finally completed in 1917, the year of the Revolution.

After the Revolution the new Soviet government eliminated all unnecessary frills and instituted a system of 'hard', 'soft' and 'international' categories of comfort. It was the open wooden carriages of the 'hard' class that carried the peasants, workers, technicians and engineers who came to develop the barren lands of Siberia.

Restaurants on wheels

Above: Space in the kitchens was at a premium. In an area of 10 square metres or less the staff had to cook dozens of four- or five-course meals to the standards of a high-class restaurant. There had to be room for a sink for washing up, and storage space for fresh food, drink, tableware and cutlery.

Below: On some of the great American transcontinental expresses the large catering staff of chefs, kitchen hands, waiters and stewards completed the whole journey on board the train. Sleeping quarters were provided for the crew, though in the early days they had to spend the nights in hammocks slung between the tables. In Europe it was usual for the crews, and even the restaurant cars themselves, to be changed at frequent intervals on a long journey.

Railway companies all over the world took a great deal of trouble to provide their passengers with a wide variety of food and drink. In America the Pullman company set the pattern. Its first dining car in 1868 was named *Delmonico* after one of New York's most famous restaurants. Featuring gas lights, a huge ice chest and hot-water heating, it could seat 48 passengers. There was a crew of two cooks and four waiters who could serve up to 250 multi-course meals per day.

Dining cars became larger and service more elaborate as time went on. In the heyday of the Broadway Limited the staff included a steward, assistant steward, chef, three cooks and ten waiters. Passengers could choose from a menu of 24 different dishes. Regional dishes became an added attraction. The Baltimore and Ohio became famous for its corn bread and country

sausage breakfasts. The Union Pacific was known for its Kansas City steaks.

Separate dining cars were usual in Britain, though on some luxury trains meals were served at every seat. On these trains the passengers spent the whole trip in comfortable armchairs. At meal times the waiters spread a linen cloth and served them the best of British food. Even on the one-hour run of the Brighton Belle a peckish commuter could sample the Pullman cold plate of tongue and ham.

It was more difficult to satisfy the cosmopolitan tastes of passengers crowding into the Wagon-Lits company's international restaurant cars on European trains. Cooking staff were changed almost as often as locomotive crews but the same fine food and service were available from one end of the continent to the other.

Below: It was no easy task to serve an elegant meal as the speeding carriage swayed from side to side.

Sleeping cars

As distances were so great in the United States it is not surprising that sleeping cars went into service there before they were introduced in Europe. The concept first became popular when George Pullman converted two carriages to include sleeping accommodation. He later built his *Pioneer*, the coach which carried President Lincoln's remains to their last resting place. Like all Pullmans for the following 50 years this was a massive affair designed to sleep the largest possible number of people. During the day it resembled a conventional American open carriage with 12 sections of four seats, in pairs facing each other. At night the seats converted into lower berths while 12 more 'uppers' swung down from the high clerestory roof. Curtains around the berths provided some privacy. A ladies' lavatory was fitted at one end of the 24-metre carriage. At the other end the gentlemen had a smoking lounge with a leather bench, brass spittoons and shaving mirrors.

The berths themselves were quite roomy but some acrobatics were required to climb the rickety ladder into an upper and then undress there. During the 1930s many standard Pullmans were rebuilt as compartment cars with double staterooms as well as single-berth compartments.

Each Pullman coach carried its own porter. His job was to help passengers on board and stow their baggage. At night he shined their shoes while they slept. When he could, the porter dozed on the hard leather bench in the smoking room. But though an experienced porter needed no more than three minutes to make up a complete section he had to attend to each passenger individually and did not get much time for rest.

The life of a Wagon-Lits attendant in Europe was quite different. He was in complete charge of the 18 passengers in his compartment car. First he sorted out their tickets and saw that their reservations were in order. He then handed them customs and immigration forms and collected their passports so they would not be disturbed every time they crossed a frontier. There were 11 checks by police, railway inspectors and customs men between Paris and Milan alone so this was a service worth having. He found out the times at which each of his passengers wished to be awakened so as not to miss their destination, and before they went to sleep he could provide evening refreshments. Everything from mineral water to champagne was ready in his pantry. During the night he kept the charcoal-fired boiler stoked up so that they had hot water for their morning wash. Finally he woke them up at the appointed time and brought them breakfast in bed.

The Compagnie Internationale des Wagon-Lits et des Grands Express Europeens, to give the company its full title, saw to it that the facilities in their sleeping cars were of the highest standard. The firm found just the style of luxury it was looking for in the boudoir cars built by a colourful American ex-soldier Colonel William Mann. When Mann's 16-passenger compartment cars proved uncompetitive with Pullman's he moved to England hoping that British aristocrats would be willing to pay for the privacy and comfort of an individual bedroom. The company soon convinced the Prince of Wales to use one of these carriages for a trip to Berlin. Before long their varnished teak sleeping cars were ranging from St Petersburg to Lisbon and from Calais to Istanbul.

Below: The small single-berth sleeping compartments contained everything the traveller needed for a comfortable night's rest.

Perhaps the most luxurious of all Wagon-Lits cars were the 400 built to the decorative designs of the great French artist René Prou, who also designed the dining-room of New York's famed Waldorf-Astoria Hotel. These royal blue cars were easily distinguished by their golden lettering in several languages and the Wagon-Lits emblem painted on their sides. They generally had eight single compartments and four doubles. All the compartments were panelled from floor to ceiling in two shades of mahogany enlivened by marquetry inlays of fruits and flowers. A burnished brass luggage rack overhead was matched by other fittings of the same material.These included a retractable reading light, cushioned rings in which bottles or glasses would not rattle, an emergency alarm with directions in four languages and even a special padded hook to hang watches on.

Above: A Pullman attendant preparing one of the upper berths while passengers sit chatting on the other side of the carriage. The seats themselves could be rearranged to form the lower bank of berths.

Below: The green Pullman sleepers in the United States had a high clerestory roof which made them particularly spacious inside. The unmistakable blue and gold livery of the carriage below shows it to be one of the sleeping cars belonging to the European Wagon-Lits company.

Above: Observation platforms were a common feature of the American trans-continental expresses. Politicians seeking election to Congress or the House of Representatives hired special trains in order to use these platforms on whistle-stop tours around their home state. Crowds turned up at every station to listen to a brief speech from the candidate, who was then whisked off to the next town for another speech.

Watching the world go by

To cope with the boredom of long-distance travel, and to provide their first-class passengers with a social focal point, the railway companies began to add lounge and observation cars to their luxury trains. They were comfortably furnished with armchairs, sofas and coffee tables. Often there was a small library of popular classics. At the end of the carriage there was usually an open observation platform from which to watch the world go by. Politicians made the most of these platforms. They were ideal places from which to deliver a speech, and Presidential candidates made whistle-stop campaign tours covering thousands of kilometres.

Franklin Roosevelt rented the carriage *Ferdinand*

Below: Coats of arms of some railway companies. 1. The American Baltimore and Ohio company included the Capitol building in Washington D.C. on their coat of arms. 2. The Union Pacific Railroad linked Chicago with the Pacific coast at California. 3. The Great Northern Railway included a mountain goat on its coat of arms.

1

2

3

Magellan from the Pullman company when he was still Governor of New York. He continued to use it as an official vehicle after becoming President of the United States, and it was re-named US Railway Car No. 1. It had four bedrooms, a dining room, kitchen, lounge and open platform. When war broke out it was given a layer of 16-mm armour plate, 75-mm bullet-proof windows and reinforced safety and emergency equipment which increased its weight to an amazing 142 tons. This made it unpopular with the train crews but it served through the Truman and Eisenhower administrations of the late 1940s before being replaced by a speedy Air Force transport.

All railway companies tried to attract new customers with gimmicks of one sort or another. The Pennsylvania Railroad, for instance, installed radios with earphones on its Broadway Limited as early as 1922. The Wagon-Lits company converted several of its dining cars to dancing cars. They were equipped with a piano and a bar, and ran regularly on the Simplon and Pullman Cote d'Azur trains. On the Golden Arrow the Trianon Bar served the international clientele travelling between London and Paris with a range of aperitifs and cocktails.

Even more British in outlook and tradition were the club cars provided for commuters. The original idea came from Lancashire textile magnates with offices in Manchester and homes in coastal resorts 60 or 70 kilometres away. Only members were admitted to these cars and membership was very strictly limited. Each member had his own leather armchair with an immaculate copy of *The Times* or the *Manchester Guardian* at hand. A discreet waiter was there to bring whatever refreshments these gentlemen desired.

Open platforms were pleasant places to ride in good weather even though there was always a chance of getting a cinder in the eye from the locomotive ahead. But as train speeds increased they were replaced by air-conditioned streamlined observation cars. The Milwaukee Road had an enclosed observation car on its fast-running Hiawatha. This was introduced in the early 1930s and featured rear windows extending far up into the roof. The same line attracted passengers on to its scenic route across to the Pacific with a double-decked Super Dome car. It had seats for 68 under a tall glass canopy, with a lounge and bar on a lower level.

Open-platform observation cars were never used in Britain. Luxury trains usually featured buffet cars, and on the beautiful Kyle of Lochalsh line in Scotland passengers on the slow-moving train could look out through three huge curved plate-glass windows which stretched almost from floor to ceiling around the end of the train. Beaver-tailed observation cars were designed by Sir Nigel Gresley for the high-speed train inaugurated in 1937 to celebrate the coronation of King George VI. Streamlined from end to end, the Coronation raced from London to Edinburgh in six hours flat, occasionally hitting speeds over 160 km/h.

Above: On long trips the bar provided refreshments and a change of company for the first-class passengers. Some railways ran exclusive club cars which only admitted carefully selected members. Everything was done to make the luxury trains resemble an expensive hotel, not just a means of transport.

The height of luxury

The ultimate in passenger comfort was provided by the magnificent private cars built for railway executives, heads of state or other VIPs. George Pullman had a special carriage built for his own personal use. These private carriages reached a peak of ostentation in the late nineteenth century when the Mann company rented glittering rolling homes to stage and opera stars such as Lily Langtry and Adeline Patti. Their owners' names were often emblazoned in elaborate gilt lettering on their sides. The interiors were usually divided into a saloon with observation platform, three or four bedrooms and a section to hold the kitchen and crew's quarters. Patti's coach boasted walls covered with embossed leather decorated with morning glory flowers outlined in gold and silver leaf. The separate bathroom was fitted out with a solid silver tub.

Many private coaches were built in America during the prosperous 1920s. Railways and other wealthy corporations thought nothing of spending $100,000 to enable their executives to enjoy the comforts of home on their business trips. The top company bosses even used these carriages to take their families on Florida vacations.

In Europe private carriages usually belonged to royalty. Queen Victoria had set the fashion when she acquired her first royal coach in 1845. In 1869 the London and North Western Railway provided her with an elaborate saloon which she used throughout the rest of her long reign. The coach built for her successor, King Edward VII, remained in service for over 50 years.

Below: The French and British flags decorated the locomotive which hauled the royal train bringing the king and queen of England to the great Paris exhibition of 1937.

Above: Train travel in India during the days of British rule sometimes included lunch by the trackside for the most privileged passengers.

King George V added bathing facilities while George VI replaced the sterling silver tub with a more modest and practical ceramic one. During his brief reign King Edward VIII preferred to borrow the office car belonging to Lord Stamp, chairman of the London Midland and Scottish Railway. In Republican France the Wagon-Lits company sold three of its luxurious parlour cars to the railways. After suitable conversion they were put at the disposal of the president in a special train which included other sleeping cars and a special restaurant car with a long central table.

The Indian railways were built by the country's British rulers as a means of unifying the vast subcontinent. The network stretched from the Khyber Pass in the west to Burma in the east and from the foothills of the Himalayas as far south as Ceylon. It used a broad 1.68-metre gauge on the trunk lines and a 1-metre or 61-centimetre gauge on feeder lines where the traffic was not so heavy. Construction was spurred on by a guaranteed 5% return to investors. By the 1920s the railways had become India's largest single employer and their tracks extended over 100,000 kilometres.

In India any passenger could hire a private coach for eight times the price of an ordinary first-class fare. Many colonial administrators and government officials did just this for their annual trips to and from the summer capital at Simla. Sportsmen and tourists travelling with the travel agent Thomas Cook used them to go on tiger hunts or to visit the Taj Mahal.

The rented carriages were often two-storey affairs with kitchens and servants' quarters below and a bedroom, sitting/dining room and bath above. The servants could take their passengers' order for lunch or dinner and fling it out of the moving train to a waiting attendant. The order was telegraphed ahead and it was not unusual to see a maharaja and his suite of red-coated British officers sitting down beside the tracks to an elaborate meal served on immaculate linen.

Winner takes all

In Britain there were two main routes for the traffic to Scotland. The west coast route ran via the industrial midlands to Glasgow, while the other route went through York, Newcastle and along the east coast to Edinburgh. There was intense competition between the two railway companies, which reached a peak when the Forth Bridge was opened. The rival trains raced to a junction a few kilometres from Aberdeen. Here the loser had to stop for signals while the winner entered the station in a triumphant cloud of steam. For a time the two companies agreed to adopt the same $8\frac{1}{4}$-hour schedule, though the rivalry continued until well after the railway companies were re-organized in 1923.

Right: A favourite sight of Rheingold passengers was the magnificent gothic cathedral beside Cologne station.

Above: The London and North Eastern Railway's Flying Scotsman service ran non-stop from London to Edinburgh. In order to allow the engine crews to change over mid-way there was a small corridor in the tender linking the footplate of the A4 Pacific with the front coach.

Above: For the first few kilometres of the return trip from Chicago to New York the Broadway Limited of the Pennsylvania Railroad ran side by side with the 20th Century Limited of the New York Central. The name 'limited' applied to the number of stops the trains made and to the number of passengers.

The same sort of competition existed on the run from the North Sea to the Alps. In 1928 the Edelweiss and Rheingold expresses were introduced between The Netherlands and Switzerland. The Edelweiss was a luxury all-Pullman aimed at businessmen rather than tourists. It left Amsterdam at 7.25 each morning. After stops at The Hague and Rotterdam it picked up British passengers at Antwerp before continuing on to Brussels, Luxembourg, Metz and Strasbourg. Its destination was Basle where it arrived at 6.38 p.m.

The German Railways' Rheingold also ran daily from the Netherlands to Basle. It started from a dockside track at the Hook of Holland where the Channel ferries from Harwich arrived. At Rotterdam it crossed paths with the Edelweiss and then ran east to Arnhem where the Dutch crew and locomotive were replaced by a German crew aboard a sleek, cone-nosed Bavarian s3/6 Pacific. There was another engine change at Mannheim, 430 kilometres farther down the line, then a fast 270 km run along the Rhine and across the Swiss border to its destination.

In America the battle was between the Pennsylvania Railroad's Broadway Limited and the New York Central's 20th Century Limited on the 1,500 kilometres separating New York from Chicago. Both trains were so popular that extra sections were run every day. At New York's Pennsylvania station, sections of the Broadway Limited's maroon and gold sleeping cars were lined up like ranks of glittering guardsmen. A powerful K4 Pacific hauled them under the Hudson River and to Philadelphia in $1\frac{1}{2}$ hours, then westward over the Allegheny mountains and around Horseshoe Curve to Pittsburgh, Cleveland and Chicago.

Meanwhile, at Grand Central station, the red carpet was out for the passengers of the 20th Century Limited. Promptly at 2.45 p.m. the first 13-car section left the station. It was electrically hauled as far as Harmon where a New York Central 4-6-4 Hudson took over for the run up the river to Albany and Schenectady. Continuing along the water-level route, it followed the Great Lakes to Buffalo, Cleveland and Toledo to reach Chicago the next day at 9.19 a.m.

Left: An electrically hauled express emerges from the Simplon tunnel. The Franco-Crosti boiler on the Italian steam engine achieved fuel savings of up to 20% using the pre-heaters beside the boiler.

Across the mountains

The line across Australia's featureless Nullarbor Plain runs for 478 kilometres without a hill or curve. If all lines could be built as straight and flat as this, engine drivers would have an easy life. Every bend tends to slow a train down and an engine can obviously pull much more weight on the level than it can on a steep incline.

Laying a track across ordinary hill country is not too hard. Carefully measured curves and a series of cuttings and embankments are used to make a track which is as straight and level as possible. But mountain ranges such as the Alps, the Rockies or the Andes are a different matter. Complicated feats of civil engineering are needed to drive a railway through this sort of terrain.

The shortest route from northern France to Italy runs through Switzerland. Crack expresses such as the Simplon-Orient and the Paris-Rome-Brindisi ran alongside Lake Geneva and up the Rhone valley as far as Brig. There they entered the 20 kilometre long Simplon tunnel. It was completed in 1906 after 11 years of digging through crumbling shale and steel-hard granite. At the time it was the world's longest rail tunnel. A second Simplon bore was completed in 1922 and was electrified from the start.

At Kicking Horse Pass in the Rockies the Canadian Pacific first laid its tracks at an improbable gradient of 1 in 23. In 1920, after 25 years of hard work, it was reduced to 1 in 45 by building a series of spiral tunnels to gain altitude. It still took two huge 2-10-4 engines

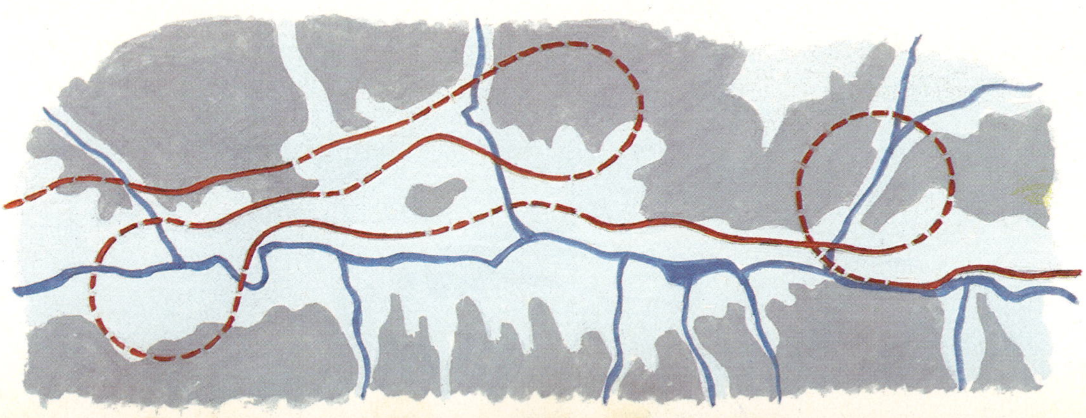

Left: A series of spiral tunnels allows the track to gain height in a short distance.

Right: A Garratt locomotive crossing the Victoria Falls bridge, 128 metres above the seething waters of the Zambezi.

Right: Even on the well-travelled west coast line to Scotland double heading was necessary to get heavy trains over the Shap incline south of Carlisle. Extra locomotives waited at such places as Tebay and Carnforth to meet this need.

teamed together to haul 900-ton passenger trains over the mountains. Two of these giant locomotives working together through the same tunnel made life very unpleasant for the crews. They had to keep their goggles down and their bandanas up over their noses to avoid being asphyxiated.

The Andes are even higher and steeper than the Rockies. When American engineer Henry Meiggs laid out the Central Railway of Peru, he had to include many tall trestle bridges over gaping chasms to reach the dizzy height of 4,830 metres at La Cima pass between Lima and Oroya. To breathe at this altitude the passengers and crew were provided with oxygen masks. Even with a ruling gradient of 1 in 23 the line needed 21 switchbacks on the 210-kilometre route. At each switchback the train ran into a siding. There it waited, often with its locomotive on the brink of a cliff, while the points were switched allowing it to continue up to the next switchback. Trains averaged only 34 km/h on this line.

The Princely Path

In the early 1920s Britain's Southern Railway publicized its Continental special as 'The Princely Path to Paris'. The French called it *la ligne luxueuse vers Londres*. There were difficult changes from train to ship and back again at Dover and Calais. The combination of boat and train often ran up to three hours late.

This situation improved in 1926 when Britain and France co-operated to inaugurate the luxury all-Pullman Golden Arrow service between their two capitals. Drawn by a sleek, green-painted *Lord Nelson* or *King Arthur* class locomotive, the train pulled out of Victoria Station promptly at 11 a.m. each day. The passengers were comfortably installed in well-upholstered armchairs inside the chocolate-and-cream coloured Pullman carriages. Passport and customs formalities were handled on board the train, so that within 17 minutes of their arrival in Dover the passengers were aboard the special cross-Channel steamer *Canterbury* and setting out for France. At the Calais Maritime terminus a Bréville Pacific was waiting, decked out with the British Union Jack and the French Tricolour and sporting the proud *Flèche d'or* symbol on its smokebox. Within minutes it too was on its way non-stop to Paris, arriving there at 5.35 p.m.

Still more convenient for those who preferred to travel at night and do business during the day was the Night Ferry service which went into operation in 1936. On this train passengers leaving Paris or London settled down for the night in luxurious sleeping cars. They could then enjoy an uninterrupted night's rest from departure to destination. This service was made possible by new train ferries equipped with a tracked deck to handle railway carriages. Special docks were built to cope with the rise and fall of the tides. A set of narrow sleeping cars was needed to match the British loading gauge, which is far smaller than the continental one. Accommodations and fittings on these 18 carriages were of the same high standard of elegance as on Europe's other blue-painted Wagon-Lits. But by each bunk the baggage net contained one piece of equipment not found elsewhere: a tested and trustworthy British standard life jacket.

The Night Ferry was not the only train to take to the water. Regular freight services also operated across the North Sea between Zeebrugge in Belgium and Harwich. Farther east, passengers and freight shared the ships crossing the Baltic from northern Germany to Denmark and Sweden. To the south the Italian State Railways carried passengers over the Straits of Messina to Sicily.

Locomotives hauling the boat trains carried special boards on their smokebox doors.

Left: The cross-Channel ferries were like small carriage sheds. Two tracks led on to the ship and branched out into four sidings for the sleeping cars.

Above: Flat access is needed to get railway vehicles on and off a ship. Special docks had to be built at Dover and Dunkirk to handle the Night Ferry. Small tank locomotives shunted the carriages on and off the ferries, trying to be as quiet as possible so as not to disturb the sleeping passengers.

Below: Passengers boarding the Pullman coaches of the Golden Arrow at London's Victoria station. On the return trip passengers were served traditional English tea from a silver service.

Up against the weather

Above: Steam-powered rotary snow ploughs had their own engines to drive the impeller blades but needed another locomotive to push them forward. Small snow drifts could be cleared with fixed snow ploughs mounted on the front of an ordinary locomotive.

Winter weather can be a misery or worse to an engine driver. Visibility is often poor, signals and points freeze up and the train may even be completely stopped. In mountainous areas like the Alps or the Rockies special snow sheds were built to protect the tracks against snow drifts and avalanches.

Snow can be a problem even in flat country. One winter evening in 1929 the eastbound Orient Express encountered a heavy snow storm not long after crossing the Turkish frontier. A drift taller than the engine itself blocked the way. The driver tried to reverse back to the last station but the blizzard was so fierce that the train was soon stuck, miles from anywhere. Within an hour the entire train was covered with snow and the outside temperature had fallen to 20 degrees below zero. There was only enough food on board for two days, and the next morning a combined expedition of railwaymen and passengers struggled through the drifts to a nearby village in search of supplies. Hurrying back over their own fast-disappearing footsteps with a few eggs, a couple of chickens and a live sheep, they were set upon by a pack of wolves. The wolves made short work of the sheep, but one of the passengers had a rifle handy and for the next two days wolf steaks and chops were served in the dining car of the crack international express. Ten days later the bank of snow was finally conquered by a heavy American snow plough. The train was able to

limp on at 10 km/h and finally arrived at its destination 15 days late.

Tropical storms can also mean trouble. On 21 September 1938 a special train on the New York, New Haven and Hartford line left Grand Central station at 12.10 p.m. Most of the passengers were boarding school boys returning from summer holiday and the platform was crowded with parents waving their children good-bye. The special eased out of the long tunnel under Park Avenue and across the Hell's Gate bridge, then picked up speed through the suburbs. The skies were growing darker and rain was beating heavily against the cab's windows, but that was nothing too unusual for the time of year. The driver pulled down his goggles, leaned out of the window and saw the signal giving him a clear track through Stamford and Bridgeport to New Haven. Here he learned that hurricane-force winds were at that moment pummelling the Atlantic shore of Long Island. Getting a green light on to the track for Providence and Boston, he gave a blast on the whistle and eased the regulator open. Crossing the Thames at New London he noticed that the water in the river was exceptionally high. Huge waves were pounding at the stout piers supporting the bridge as he reduced speed for the yellow caution signal just before the long causeway across the shallow bay to Stonington.

But the hurricane had beaten him to it. The power of the wind-driven waves had begun to wash away the ballast from the rock-fill causeway. Though moving at only a snail's pace, he could feel the track begin to tilt under the weight of the heavy engine. He had no choice but to stop completely with the train stranded over a kilometre from the shore. Dispatching his fireman for help, he set his brakes and blew off excess steam before walking calmly back along the train. After organizing the conductors and porters and reassuring his young passengers he led them in single file through the shoulder-deep water to the safety of the shore. During the night the train capsized and the causeway was swept away.

Below: Though the train eventually toppled into the water, no lives were lost in this autumn storm in New England in 1938.

Accident!

Railway accidents were extremely rare, and deaths and injuries were much less frequent than with any other form of transport. But a derailed train of telescoped cars along a torn up track, or an engine lying on its side belching steam and smoke made a spectacular sight. Human errors such as excessive speed or failure to observe signals were often to blame for accidents. Mechanical failures also occurred despite the increasingly ingenious safety devices incorporated in most trains.

Over 200 lives were lost in an accident on the Caledonian line which resulted from a signalman's mistake. A fully laden troop train rammed the rear of a passenger train on a siding. The wrecked trains were struck then in turn by an oncoming express. Five hundred people were killed near Modane in the French Alps when the engine of an express routed through the Mont Cenis tunnel plunged off the track and down an embankment. The train was heavily overloaded at the time and its brakes were unable to slow its descent down the steep slope despite all the driver's efforts.

There were often collisions with road vehicles on level-crossings, and ice-bound points could easily derail a train. Occasionally a driverless, runaway engine travelled 30 kilometres or more before finally running out of steam.

Track-maintenance operations were also a source of danger. On a British line a maintenance team replacing ballast accidentally left a raised jack under a rail as a train approached. Despite its reduced speed, the train was nearly flipped over.

One of the greatest causes of delays on the railways was the 'hot-box', or faulty bearing on one of the axles of a locomotive or carriage. Hot-boxes were caused by faulty lubrication, loose or worn journal liners or sub-standard bearings. Loose threads in the lubricating pads sometimes worked their way up into the bearing surface. Cinders or grit could filter into the axle-box if the lid was accidently left open. Most hot-boxes were detected in time by their characteristic smell or by the oily black smoke pouring from them. When this happened the train was stopped and the defective unit was doused with cold water. The oil sump was then refilled before the train was allowed to proceed. But if a failure remained undetected it could be deadly at high

Axle box

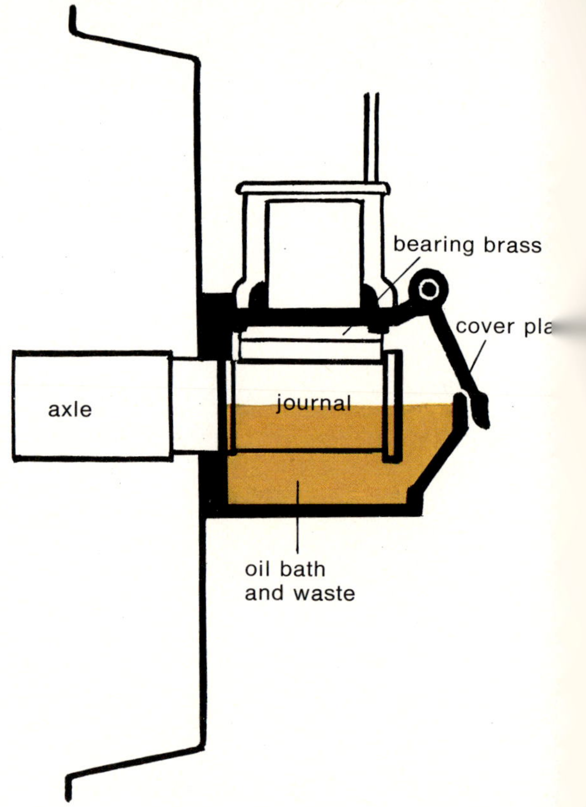

speed. Once the Congressional Limited, travelling at 100 km/h, suffered such a failure between New York and Washington. The toll was 79 dead and 129 injured. The hot-box problem was reduced with regular inspection and the installation of electric detection devices. It was virtually eliminated when roller bearings were introduced on the new streamlined coaches which appeared in the 1930s.

All-steel carriages which would not telescope had by then long replaced the old fire-prone wooden cars. The interlock system of signalling eliminated many of the dangers from incorrectly set points and signals. But little or nothing could be done to prevent vandalism or sabotage. When a section of track across the Nevada desert was secretly tampered with one day in 1939, the crack City of San Francisco plunged over the embankment at top speed. The Union Pacific Railroad immediately brought in a huge crane to clear the tracks and remove the debris, and a track-laying crew soon followed. Nevertheless 24 people were killed.

Despite such disasters only 370 lives were lost in railway accidents in the United States between 1918 and 1939. On a passenger-mile basis the railways remained the safest form of transportation on land or sea or in the air.

Left: The tapered end of the axle on each wheel was machined to provide a journal. This supported the weight of the vehicle through a bronze half-bearing, called a 'brass', fitted with a white-metal insert. The lower part of the journal box formed an oil sump. It contained loose heavy thread or 'waste' which applied a thin film of oil to the journal as it turned.

Left: Huge steam-driven cranes were used to lift damaged carriages and locomotives on to the track after an accident.

Left: In 1929 Mexican irregular troops under Gonzalo Escobar seized a train. But the rebellion was eventually put down when government forces of President Obregon regained control.

Railways at war

The surge of railway construction in the nineteenth century caused as great a revolution in military strategy as it did in the civilian economy. Troops were first carried by rail during the Crimean War. During the American Civil War, General Sherman's advance across the South only became possible after he had cleared the tracks of Confederate soldiers. He then used the railway to bring forward his own troops and supplies.

In Europe the Prussian general staff was always consulted on the location of all new lines being built. By 1914 Germany had a network of strategic railways along its northern and western frontiers. When the First World War broke out, the German plans to capture France within a few weeks failed largely because the Belgian army blew up tracks, tunnels and bridges as it retreated. The invading German forces had to advance on foot and this gave the British army time to reach the battle front by rail.

In Italy the decision to defend the Piave was in part dictated by the good rail connections there. Four British and six French divisions were rushed to this vital sector in over 1,400 separate trains run by French and Italian railways crews. On the Western Front thousands of kilometres of narrow-gauge track were laid down

Right: Russian operation of the Manchurian railway was one of the causes of the Boxer Rebellion at the turn of the century. Even thirty years later bandits stopped the trains and burned the luxurious teak carriages still operating on the line.

immediately behind the trenches to bring up men and supplies. Special ambulance trains marked with red crosses were fitted out with operating facilities and racks for stretchers.

Camouflaged armoured trains protected munitions depots and troop concentrations. Big guns like the Big Bertha used to shell Paris were mounted on railway bogies. They were aimed by manoeuvring them on curved sections of the track.

Many railway workers were killed or injured by shrapnel from exploding shells or machine-gun bullets from strafing enemy fighters. In the Second World War marshalling yards became prime targets for high-flying bombers.

Left: The Red Army's armed trains played an important role in the Russian Civil War of 1919-21.

The great termini

At first railway stations consisted of nothing more than a waiting room, a ticket office and a platform beside a single track. As more and more people began to travel by rail, stations became more elaborate. A barn-like structure was often built over the tracks to shelter passengers from the weather.

As traffic increased more tracks and platforms were required. The original wooden sheds were replaced by vast steel and glass vaults. These not only kept the rain out but also allowed steam and smoke from the engine to escape upward through vents in the roof. London's St Pancras station was opened in 1868. A beautiful steel and glass shed spanned the platforms in a single parabolic arch 73 metres wide. The station frontage was enhanced by a red-brick gothic-style facade which housed the Midland Hotel. By the end of the nineteenth century Philadelphia's Broad Street station boasted of a vault soaring over 90 metres in a single span.

Even more impressive was the series of five interconnected translucent vaults designed by Italian architect Ulisse Stacchini for the new station in Milan. Built between 1923 and 1931 it rivalled the city's cathedral in size. Its train sheds were backed by a huge complex of halls and concourses with inlaid mosaic floors and a maze of grandiose staircases. Passengers had to walk a long way to reach the platform after entering the station through the imposing marble frontage.

These vast concourses and waiting rooms were needed to accommodate the thousands of people passing through the station each day. As well as the offices used by passengers buying tickets and checking their baggage there had to be space for the friends and relatives who came to see them off. Some people came just to make the most of the shops, restaurants and news-stands, some of which stayed open night and day. Most large stations also had their own hotels either within the station buildings or situated close by.

Railway companies and municipal authorities joined to make every main station an impressive gateway to the city. At New York's Pennsylvania Station the fluted columns and caissoned ceilings were modelled on the vast baths of Carracala in ancient Rome. The ceiling of the concourse at Grand Central, New York's other main station, was painted dark blue and was completed with twinkling stars. The central octagonal information booth was surmounted by a four-faced golden clock which became a meeting place for people from all over

Above: Grand Central station in New York was completed in 1913. It covered over 20 hectares and contained 44 platforms and 67 tracks on two underground levels. Grand Central became the busiest terminal in the world, handling 550 trains and 180,000 passengers on an average day.

Left: A driver's-eye view of the tracks entering Central station, Milan. Like many other main termini, Milan Central was open for 24 hours a day to deal with local services as well as international expresses. It is still one of Europe's most important stations though most of the traffic is now electrically hauled.

the world. Straddling New York's Park Avenue, Grand Central was an important city landmark. The imposing facade was topped by another great clock decorated with an American eagle and a statue of Mercury, the ancient Greek god of communications.

Even the smallest country station had its clock. A special service in every railway administration ensured that every timepiece, from the drivers' pocket watches to the shed and station clocks, showed precisely the same time. The expression 'by the station clock' became a synonym for chronological accuracy.

Maintenance and overhaul

When the driver left his locomotive at the end of a trip he had to fill out a complete report. This included observations on the locomotive's performance and any incidents on the journey. His working day was then over and he could go home and get cleaned up.

Meanwhile the locomotive had been taken over by a maintenance crew. After the empty coaches had been pulled away to the carriage sheds they backed off the locomotive into the depot. The first stop was over a pit where its fire was dumped. Just enough steam was left in the boiler for it to move to its allotted siding in the shed.

Despite its imposing bulk, a steam locomotive was a piece of precision equipment. Its parts were liable to wear or to damage by dirt or corrosion. The maintenance crew's first job was therefore to clean the engine from top to bottom. They used long-handled fire irons to chip clinker from the grate, for if it was allowed to build up it could impede the draught or block the damper. Then they flushed out the fire-tubes with steam, cleaned the smokebox and inspected the blast pipe and chimney to ensure they were completely free of soot. Each pipe fitting also had to be carefully checked for leaks, and washers were replaced when necessary.

Routine daily maintenance and inspection operations were supplemented by periodic overhauls. Particular attention was paid to the boiler to ensure that there was no chance that it would burst. At regular intervals the locomotive was completely dismantled and rebuilt with new or refurbished parts. Well-designed and properly maintained locomotives could remain in service for 50 years or more.

Each locomotive was individually built even if it was part of a large series. Every one of its moving parts was

Below: Finding adequate supplies of mineral-free water was a problem for railwaymen everywhere. The main-line Garratts of southern Africa needed the contents of both tender tanks for trips across the desert.

Left: Cleaning out the fire-tubes was one of the dirtiest jobs on the railways. It had to be done every day.

numbered. Defective parts were not simply thrown away and replaced by new ones. A worn bearing or bent connecting rod on a locomotive would be painstakingly re-bored or re-aligned. The railway companies all had well-equipped repair shops where this work was done. They were noisy, cavernous buildings filled with a vast array of drills, presses, milling machines and enormous lathes. They usually included a foundry where new parts were cast from hot metal. Huge overhead gantry cranes were used to lift the 100-ton locomotives off their wheels.

Craftsmen with many different skills were employed there but perhaps the most important were the boiler and fire-tube specialists. There were two related factors which could prevent an engine steaming properly – soot inside the fire-tubes and scale outside. Both had to be removed from time to time. Cleaning and scraping the tubes was certainly the dirtiest job on the railways. Chipping away the hundreds of pounds of rock-hard, crystalline scale which accumulated around the tubes was an even harder task but an equally vital one. A build-up of scale between the closely packed tubes could prevent the water from circulating freely and thus absorb heat. Moreover the scale was chemically corrosive and could eat through the metal, making a major overhaul necessary and immobilizing the engine for weeks. The railways' mechanical engineers were well aware of this problem. Each had his own secret recipe for preventing scale formation and many added special ingredients to the water in the tender.

Below: Some of the tools used to maintain the locomotives including the driver's oil cans and three long fire irons used to chip away the clinker.

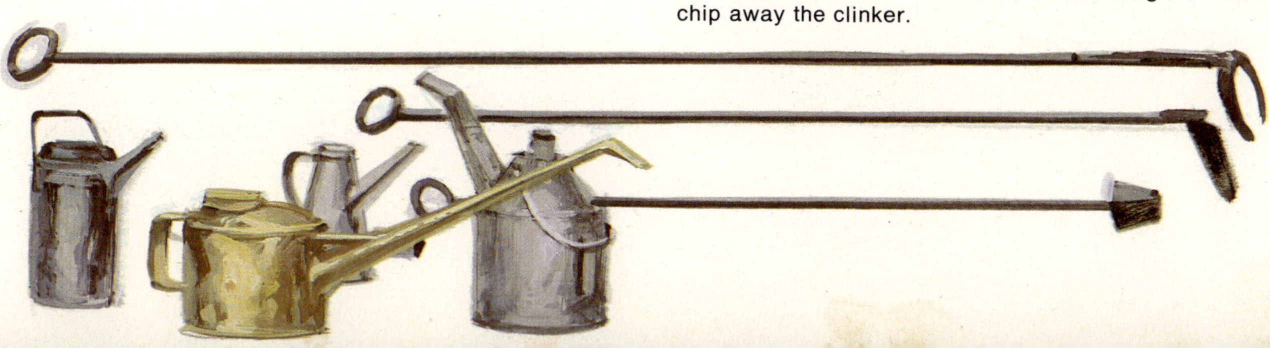

A home from home

Long-distance trains and special schedules often left engine crews a long way from their home depots at the end of their spell of duty. Most railway companies ran hostels for their staff at intermediate points along every main line. Some of them were modern buildings with central heating and individual cubicles. But many more were rough barracks built close to the train sheds, often inside the railway yard itself. Most of them were noisy and dirty and were heated by nothing more than a small coke stove. They often became extremely crowded at peak periods. Yet there was great pride and companionship between the footplate crews.

Tired and dirty from a long day's run the driver and fireman turned their locomotive over to the maintenance crew before signing off duty. Pushing into the hostel they greeted old friends and got them to save a couple of seats at the crowded mess table before heading off towards the sinks for a thorough scrub.

After the evening meal it would be time to relax and tell stories, play cards or draughts, discuss union affairs or even take a brief stroll into the town. French railwaymen might recall the time when a president of France fell out of a moving train. Leaving Paris one warm spring evening in 1920 Paul Deschanel opened the window wide to get some air into his stuffy compartment. Ignoring the sign which warned 'Do not lean out of the window', he tumbled on to the ballast in his pyjamas. He was shaken but unhurt and managed to stagger to a crossing-keeper's cottage. He could not prove his identity but was nevertheless given a glass of warm milk and put to bed. It was five hours before the driver was told that a man had fallen out of his train. He set off to inspect the carriages but did not look inside the president's compartment as he did not want to disturb such an important man. It was another two hours before railway officials realized that the crossing keeper's guest was actually the president of the republic.

About 15 years later another event became the talk of the French railways. It was a sequel to the Stavisky scandal in which members of the government were found to have been involved in corrupt financial deals. One morning some maintenance men patrolling a section of the Paris–Dijon line found the body of a member of the official tribunal which had been investigating the case. He had been tied hand and foot across the track and a train had run him over during the night.

As evening wore on in the hostel, conversation died down as the men prepared to get some rest. They slept in crowded dormitories in which the driver and fireman usually tried to get bunks close together. It was hard to get a full night's sleep. Starting from the small hours, crews were getting up to go on duty. Those who remained behind could hear the shriek of locomotive whistles and the noise of trains from the yards nearby. A young apprentice usually had the job of waking the crews up in time to go on duty. If he was new to the job he had to wake up half a dozen men or more before finding the right ones.

Eventually the time came to go back on duty. After backing the locomotive into the station and coupling up with their train the driver and fireman waited once again for the all-clear for the journey home. If they were lucky there would be time for a makeshift meal. The fireman cleaned off his shovel with the steam hose and placed a couple of sausages or rashers of bacon on it. Opening the firebox door he rested the shovel on the glowing coals, and before long a tasty fried breakfast was ready for him and the driver.

The next night they would be able to sleep in their own beds at home with their families. But though home comforts were always welcome, most drivers enjoyed the occasional night away in the company of their workmates at the railway hostel.

Right: One of the complex steam whistles which some American drivers fitted to their locomotives to give them their own distinctive sound. Most locomotives were fitted with much simpler standard whistles.

Above: The railwaymen's hostels were often dingy and uncomfortable. Nevertheless they could be friendly places where old friends met and chatted for an hour or two over their food. The men rested on simple wooden bunks but were lucky to get much sleep as other crews came and went throughout the night.

Record breakers

In the early 1930s the world air-speed record was raised to over 700 km/h and Sir Malcolm Campbell's car pushed the land-speed record over the 400 km/h mark. Streamlining became an obsession with the public and even locomotive designers were affected. Fast diesel trains like Germany's Flying Hamburger or the American Burlington Zephyr were reaching 200 km/h on the flat.

There was still plenty of enthusiasm for steam, and British designers revamped their old machines and produced new ones to speed the express schedules again and again. Big streamlined Pacifics drawing strings of passenger coaches roared north from London to reach Newcastle in four hours and to Edinburgh in six. Sir Nigel Gresley designed the A4 class of streamlined Pacifics for the London and North Eastern Railway. The last four of the class were further improved by the Kylchap exhaust system. On 3 July 1938, Gresley A4 No. 4468 *Mallard* set up a new world speed record for steam. Pulling a dynamometer car it travelled at 203 km/h – a record which remains unbeaten to this day.

To inaugurate its high-speed Hiawatha service between Chicago and Minneapolis in 1935, the Milwaukee railway designed a completely new train as an integrated unit. It consisted of seven stainless-steel cars painted with a bright orange stripe, hauled by a mammoth streamlined Atlantic locomotive built especially for express work. This was the largest engine of its type ever built. It was so successful in meeting its designed speed of 160 km/h that further coaches were added to the luxury express without reducing its speed.

The New York Central commissioned industrial

Hiawatha

20th Century Limited

designer Henry Dreyfuss to re-design the prestigious 20th Century Limited. He produced a new style for everything on the train from its coffee spoons to the bullet nose of its powerful 4-6-4 Hudson engine.

The mid-1930s also saw the development of steam turbine locomotives. The first of these had bulky condensers like those used on ships but later non-condensing types successfully hauled coal in Sweden and the Appalachians. Sir William Stanier produed a beautiful passenger version for Britain's London Midland and Scottish Railway.

Borsig 5001

Below: Firemen found it almost impossible to satisfy the appetite for coal of such massive engines as the Pennsylvania Railroad's 4,000-hp K4s. Eventually all large American locomotives were fitted with mechanical stokers. A series of Archimedean screws fed coal from the bottom of the tender to the level of the firebox. It was blown into the grate by jets of steam.

Stanier turbine

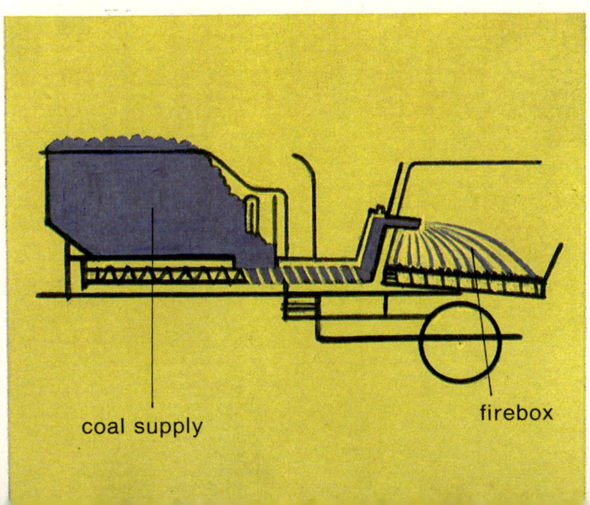

The Train Bleu

The reporters who responded to Lord Dalziel's invitation and gathered on the platforms at Calais Maritime on 9 December 1922 little realized that they were witnessing the birth of a legend. 'Look' said one, 'A blue train!' Indeed the five all-steel sleeping cars, fresh from the Forge & Co. works in Leeds, were painted dark blue below the window line and a lighter blue above. The

Left: In his elegant fur-collared coat, impressario Serge Diaghilev of the Ballets russes de Monte Carlo invariably tipped and congratulated the driver and fireman of the Train Bleu on its arrival in Monaco. He was so enthralled with this overnight express that in 1924 he commissioned Jean Cocteau and Darius Milhaud to write a ballet in its honour. It was an immediate success and spread the fame of this luxurious train still further.

Train Bleu was thus baptized. The name did not become official or appear on the destination panels on the sides of each car for over forty years. Nevertheless the Train Bleu soon became a favoured meeting place for the fashionable and famous who were making the journey from the cold and damp of the North European winters to the sunny beaches and splended casinos of the French and Italian Rivieras.

The tone was set on the inaugural journey when the Wagon-Lits company's passengers were greeted on arrival next morning by the Mayor of Nice, the Crown Prince of Sweden and the prefect of the *département* of Alpes-Maritimes. Lunch followed at the chic Ruhl Hotel and tea was served in Monte Carlo. The day ended with a formal dinner in the vast halls of the Nice casino.

The Calais-Paris-Nice express, as it appeared on the schedules, was not the first luxury train to travel to the Mediterranean. As early as the 1880s Georges Nagelmackers had organized international sleeping car service between such far-flung points as St Petersburg, Vienna, Lisbon and the Cote d'Azur. He also built the Riviera Palace Hotel in Cimiez, above Nice, where Queen Victoria spent her winters. The palm-shaded walk along the sea front in Nice became known as the Promenade des Anglais after the British lords and ladies who followed in her wake.

Until quite recently the Riviera was a winter-only resort. The Calais-Mediterranean express was curtly dismissed from the summer schedules of 1929 with the words 'Does not run in the summer.' But from November to May the wealthy and the talented crowded Platform A of the Paris Gare de Lyon to board the train to the south.

The tinkling of a silver bell summoned the passengers to the Pergola restaurant car with its vases of fresh flowers on every table. An exquisite five-course meal was served to them on gold-monogrammed white porcelain. Afterwards they retired for the night to their comfortable compartments while the sharp-eyed engine crew in their powerful PLM Pacific transported them smoothly and swiftly southward to Marseilles and the Mediterranean. After a five-minute early-morning stop in the great port city the Train Bleu raced on through the many tunnels along the coast as far as Toulon and St Raphael. It then began to deposit its celebrated passengers at half-hour intervals in Antibes, Cannes, Nice, Monte Carlo, Ventimiglia and San Remo.

Above: King Boris of Bulgaria was one of a number of royal train enthusiasts. The Spanish King Alphonso XIII also enjoyed taking a turn on the footplate of a great steam locomotive. Alphonso could call on expert help from his cousin the Duke of Segovia. The Duke held a full driver's certificate and continued to drive the Spanish railways' most powerful steam locomotives until he was 70 years old.

To the driver and fireman in the cab, the famous Train Bleu was not just another string of coaches to be delivered to its destination on schedule. It was the culmination of a career of shovelling coal and peering through the night at approaching signals. To be in charge of one of the great expresses was a supreme mark of trust and one more reason why they could never consider exchanging their own craft for any other job in the world.

Glossary

Adhesion: Friction between the rails and a locomotive's driving wheels. Low adhesion leads the driving wheels to slip.

Articulated suspension: The system in which the ends of two adjacent vehicles are supported on a common bogie. Articulated locomotives consisted of two or more separate sections supported in this way.

Atlantic: The 4-4-0 wheel arrangement.

Axle: The shaft joining a pair of wheels.

Axle box: The bearing and lubrication assembly at the end of each axle.

Ballast: The mixture of pebbles and stones on which the track is laid. The ballast spreads the load of the train across a wide area and keeps the tracks well drained.

Bearing: A component which transfers the weight of the train between two moving parts, e.g. between the wheels of a wagon and its frame.

Blast pipe: The narrow opening through which steam passes into the smokebox after leaving the cylinders. It produces a partial vacuum in the smokebox which helps to draw air through the fire-tubes.

Bogie: A small four- or six-wheeled truck which supports one end of a locomotive or carriage. On a locomotive the bogie in front of the driving wheels is called the leading bogie; the bogie behind the driving wheels is called the trailing bogie.

Boiler: The section of the locomotive in which water is turned into high-pressure steam.

Buffer: Spring-loaded stop which projects from the end of each carriage and wagon to cushion the shock when they collide.

Compound: A system in which exhaust steam from one set of cylinders is fed into a further set of cylinders before being exhausted through the chimney.

Conductor: American name for a guard.

Coupling: The equipment used to join rolling stock together. Two or three heavy links are provided at the end of each wagon. These are attached to a large hook on the next wagon to couple the two together.

Crossing-keeper: The railway worker responsible for opening and closing level-crossing gates. Crossing-keepers often lived in cottages by the crossing so as to be available day and night.

Destination boards: Boards which are fitted on to the sides of each carriage on every journey, showing its precise route and destination.

Driving wheels: The large wheels of a locomotive which are driven by the pistons.

Exhaust: The waste steam or smoke from the locomotive.

Fire-tubes: Fine tubes which run through the boiler carrying hot gases from the fire. Heat passes from the gases into the water in the boiler to produce steam.

Footplate: The area at the rear of the locomotive on which the driver and fireman stand.

Flange: The raised edge of a wheel which runs along the inside of the rails.

Gantry: A structure above the tracks which carries signals.

Gauge: The distance between a pair of rails. The standard gauge of 1.435 metres was chosen by George Stephenson. It is said to be the same as the distance between the wheels of Roman chariots. It is used throughout America and in Britain and most of Europe. In the Soviet Union the gauge is 1.524 metres, and in Spain it is 1.676 metres.

Guard: The railway official responsible for the carriages or wagons on a train and their passengers or load.

Injector: A device for forcing water from the tender into the boiler.

Kylchap: An exhaust system invented by the Finnish engineer Kyläla and perfected in France by André Chapelon.

Loading gauge: The maximum width and height of trains allowed on a certain section of track. Bridges and platforms were built to allow trains of a particular loading gauge to pass. Each country usually has a standard loading gauge for the whole of its system. Great Britain: width 2.75 m, height 3.95 m. Europe: width 3.10 m, height 4.50 m. United States: width 3.30 m, height 4.90 m. Soviet Union: width 3.40 m, height 5.30 m.

Pacific: The 4-6-2 wheel arrangement.

Points: Movable rails which allow a train to switch from one track to another. Points are usually controlled from signal boxes, but those leading to little-used sidings are operated by a lever beside the track.

Regulator: The device operated by the driver which controls the amount of steam leaving the boiler.

Right-away: The signal from the guard or station master which tells the driver that the train is ready to depart.

Rolling stock: The unpowered carriages and wagons used on the railways.

Roundhouse: A star-shaped arrangement of tracks leading from a central turntable to a series of sheds arranged in a circle.

Shunter: Railway worker who stands down on the tracks to couple carriages or wagons together.

Sleeper: Pieces of timber laid at right-angles to the track about every 50 centimetres. The rails are bolted to the sleepers to keep them the correct distance apart.

Smokebox: Space in front of the boiler where hot exhaust gases from the fire-tubes mix with steam from the blast pipe before passing up the chimney.

Snow plough: A device fitted on to the front of a locomotive to push snow off the line. Large snow ploughs have their own wheels and are pushed along by another locomotive.

Steam turbine: A series of blades which are turned by steam passing through them.

Superheater: Arrangement of tubes in front of the fire-tubes in which steam leaving the boiler is heated to higher temperature and pressure.

Tank: An engine which carries fuel and water on its own frame rather than in a separate tender.

Tender: The wagon drawn behind most steam locomotives which contains their fuel and water supplies.

Wheel arrangement: The description of the number of driving wheels and bogie wheels of steam locomotives, e.g. 4-6-2. The first figure (4) shows the number of wheels in the leading bogie while the last figure (2) shows the number of wheels in the trailing bogie. The figure in the middle (6) shows the number of driving wheels. If there is more than one separate set of driving wheels then each set is shown separately, e.g. a 4-8-8-4 has four-wheeled leading and trailing bogies and two separate sets of eight driving wheels.

Main events

1712: The Cornish mining engineer Newcomen builds a steam-driven pump.

1769: James Watt patents an improved version of Newcomen's steam engine. James Cugnot's steam-driven car runs in Paris.

1804: Richard Trevithick builds a steam locomotive.

1825: Marc Seguin and George Stephenson build a tubular boiler. Railway built between Stockton and Darlington operated by Stephenson's *Locomotion*.

1828: First French railway opens between Saint-Etienne and Andrezieux.

1830: Liverpool-Manchester railway opens and carries post between the two towns.

1834: First Belgian railway opens between Malines and Brussels.

1835: First German railway opens between Nuremburg and Fürth. First Dutch railway opens between Haarlem and Amsterdam.

1836: First Canadian railway opens from Laprairie to Saint Johns.

1838: First travelling post office enters service between Liverpool and London.

1839: First Italian railway opens between Naples and Portici.

1841: Thomas Cook organizes the world's first railway excursion.

1843: Crampton builds large-wheel locomotive.

1844: Turner paints 'Rain, Steam and Speed' depicting a railway scene.

1846: Stephenson's standard gauge of 1.435 metres adopted in Britain.

1847: First Swiss railway opens between Baden and Zurich.

1848: First Spanish railway opens between Barcelona and Mataro.

1852: First South American railway opens in Chile.

1854: First Indian railway opened. First Australian railway opened between Melbourne and Sandridge.

1856: Railways used in Crimean War to carry troops. First Russian railway opened between St Petersburg and Moscow. First Portuguese railway opened between Lisbon and Cintra.

1859: The steam injector is invented by Henry Gifford. George Pullman's first sleeping car runs between Bloomington and Chicago.

1860: The first railway in Africa opens between Durban and Point.

1863: During the American civil war 25,000 troops were transported by rail in 12 days. A restaurant car starts operating between Philadelphia and Baltimore.

1864: Square firebox introduced by Alfred Belpaire.

1869: Lines from Atlantic and Pacific coasts of America are joined at Promontory Point, Utah.

1871: The Mont-Cenis tunnel (the first alpine tunnel) is driven under the Alps. George Westinghouse perfects the automatic air brake. Nagelmackers signs his first international contract to carry passengers on the India Mail.

1872: The first Japanese railway is opened between Tokyo and Yokohama.

1876: The Compagnie International des Wagon-Lits is formed.

1879: Siemens exhibits the world's first electric locomotive in Berlin.

1882: Spiral tunnels built in Switzerland beneath the St Gothard pass.

1883: Orient Express begins operations from Paris to Varna

1884: Anatole Mallet builds the first compound articulated locomotive for the Biarritz railway.

1885: Canadian transcontinental line is completed.

1885: First four-cylinder compound built for the French Nord railway.

1887: Sud Express begins operation between Paris, Madrid and Lisbon.

1891: Construction of Trans-Siberian railway begins.

1893: The 20th Century Limited begins operations to celebrate the Chicago exhibition.

1894: Pullman workers strike. Several are killed.

1904: Ansaldo builds Zara class bogie locomotives for the Adriatic line.

1905: The Pennsylvania Railroad locomotive M7002 hauling the Broadway Limited reaches an unconfirmed speed of 205 km/h.

1906: Simplon tunnel enters service.

1907: Garratt patents his system of articulated locomotives.

1912: First diesel locomotive built in Germany.

1916: The Balwin company builds a giant Mallet 2-8-8-8-4 with six cylinders and a tractive force of 75,500 kg for the Virginia Railroad. Arturo Caprotti patents his system of poppet valves.

1917: Railway across Australia enters service.

1918: Armistice ending the First World War signed in a disused railway restaurant car.

1919: Simplon-Orient express enters service. French railway workers achieve eight-hour working day.

1922: Calais-Mediterranean express (commonly known as the Train Bleu) enters service.

1925: A 1,200-hp German diesel becomes the first to haul an express.

1925: André Chapelon perfects the Kylchap exhaust system.

1928: Rheingold express inaugurated between Hook of Holland and Basle. Edelweiss inaugurated between Amsterdam and Basle.

1929: Wagon-Lits company series Lx sleepers designed by René Prou enter service. Sunshine express enters service between Alexandria and Aswan via Cairo.

1930: The Dominion enters service covering 4,650 kilometres between the Atlantic and Pacific coast in 87 hours.

1931: First air-conditioned Pullman car enters service between Washington and New York. Turkestan-Siberia line opens between Alma-Ata and Novosibirsk.

1932: First train crosses the Sydney Harbour bridge.

1934: The 18.5 km Apennine tunnel opens on new line between Bologna and Florence.

1935: The Flying Hamburger diesel train set a world speed record of 214 km/h.

1936: Night Ferry service inaugurated between London and Paris.

1938: The London and North Eastern Railway's *Mallard* sets a world speed record for steam of 203 km/h. French railways are nationalized.

1939: Blue Train inaugurated in South Africa between Pretoria and Capetown.

Index

Numbers in *italics* refer to illustrations and captions

Europe

Aberdeen
Glasgow
Edinburgh
Flying Scotsman
Carlisle
Newcastle
Royal Scot
York
Crewe
Silver Jubilee
Rugby
Harwich
London
Exeter
Brighton
Penzance
Dover
Calais
Dunkirk
Zeebrugge
Hook of Holland
Amsterdam
Arnhem
Rotterdam
Brussels
Liege
Cologne
Rheingold
Amiens
Luxembourg
Edelweiss
Mannheim
Karlsruhe
Paris
Strasbourg
Orient Express
Munich
Basle
Dijon
Lausanne
Sud Express
Lyons
Milan
Venice
Blue Train
Bordeaux
San Remo
Nice
Ventimiglia
Monte Carlo
Cannes
Marseilles
Bologna
Florence
Rome
Naples
Palermo
Hendaye/Irun
Burgos
Madrid
Lisbon
Copenhagen
Hamburg
Flying Hamburger
Hanover
Berlin